THE BRAIN IS A BOUNDARY

THE *B*RAIN
IS A *B*OUNDARY

A Journey in Poems
to the Borderlines
of Lewy Body Dementia

Alexander Dreier

Lindisfarne Books
2016

Published by
Lindisfarne Books
610 Main Street
Great Barrington, Massachusetts 01230

ISBN: 978-1-58420-997-3

Lindisfarne Books is an imprint of
SteinerBooks | Anthroposophic Press

www.steinerbooks.org

For my wife, Olivia;
our sons, Matthew and Lucas;
and my writing mentor, Pat Schneider.

ACKNOWLEDGMENTS

My deepest, heartfelt thanks go to Pat Schneider, creator of the AWA (Amherst Writers and Artists) method, which allowed my lifelong love for words and language to flow freely onto the written page. I am also grateful for the many people with whom I have written over the years in Pat's workshops, especially Al Miller, Peter Schneider, and Suzanne Webber. Also owed a debt of gratitude for contributing to this volume are: Arthur Zajonc, (Introduction) long-time friend and the wisest person I know; Dr. Bradley Boeve, without whom I would never have been able to understand or benefit from the amazing research and treatments available to those experiencing Lewy Body Disease; Olivia, my wife, true love, and unshakeable supporter (endless help with editing and magically arranging the sequence of the poems, as well as largely co-authoring "My Life with Lewy").

I also wish to thank the editors of the journals in which the following poems first appeared: "Wild Roses" in *Passager*; "First Time," "Bring Me Along," and "At Lunch," in *Sulpher River Literary Review*; "Whole Moon Story" and "This is Awkward" in *Red Rock Review*; "Turquoise Prayer of Spring" in *RE:AL: The Journal of Liberal Arts*; "Stone Circles" in the *Hampden-Sidney Poetry Review*; "Me Not in the Photograph" in *Eclipse: A Literary Journal*; and "Who is Delivered" and "Photograph of Mother at Thanksgiving" in *Whetstone*.

Contents

THE BRAIN IS A BOUNDARY

THE UNLIKELIHOOD OF BEING

LIFE ON THE HILL

CHRONICLES OF LEWY

THRESHOLDS

Introduction

by Arthur Zajonc

MOST WHO KNOW Alexander Dreier, know him as a comedian. Few will know that, parallel with his comedic routines, Alexander has been busy crafting poems of rare tenderness and insight. For the first time, many of his poems are gathered together here in one volume. Written over a period of fifteen years, these poems cover a wide range of subject matter, but they all reflect Alexander's ability to closely observe and render whatever he experiences in original and compelling language.

My friend Alexander and I share a common malady: our brains are falling apart. His is failing due to the inclusion of Lewy bodies, while mine has largely stopped producing the neurotransmitter dopamine, which is another way of saying I am suffering from Parkinson's. Both are degenerative neurological diseases with somewhat similar symptoms, a sampling of which are on display in the section called "Chronicles of Lewy." But it would be a great mistake to suppose that this is merely a collection of poems that chronicles his disease. Most of these poems were written before his diagnosis. Yet they do largely share a common theme: the exploration of a boundary or threshold of consciousness, be it the threshold of sanity or death; or the cleft between subject and object, mind and brain; or the distance between lover and the beloved.

Consider, for instance, the title poem with its vivid description of the twin experiences of body and mind, starkly separated in the poem by a barbed wire border. On the one side glucose and hemoglobin, on the other side an "untamed lightness / of elephants treading the spirit savanna." What do biochemistry and neurology have to do with the snowy egret standing "alone, open-eyed, her beak agape to the sun"? The crossing of that deep divide in consciousness has been termed "the hard problem" by philosopher David Chalmers. It is at once the threshold between waking and sleeping, between meditative awareness and distraction, between life and death. Alexander's poems often situate themselves at the forbidden crossing where our passage is blocked, but, as he writes, where occasionally "small ones" are allowed to pass through unnoticed. These are the momentary glimpses we may have of other dimensions to our world.

The New England coast, and especially Maine, have always held a special place of affection for Alexander and his family. Where the sea pounds against granite slabs and waves lap on a stony beach, we confront a strong elemental beauty and living landscape. Here the ever-changing forces of nature rise up to meet us, calm one day and tempestuous the next. This eternally restless boundary, where ocean and land meet, figures in several poems. In "Stone Circles," for example, we learn to see that not only do we humans press wishes into magic ringed stones (a striking image) and throw them both into the sea, but the stones themselves carry a circling power. We are instructed:

Then, holding wish and stone together

in your stronger arm, throw them both

in a slowly arcing curve into the sea.

The story does not end with the toss of wish and stone. No, the stones themselves can come "crawling back to you,/ compelled by its own wish for circularity/to look you in the eye again." What an apt perception! Look longer, patiently, and you may very well see that circling power of stone and sea. Once again, at a boundary, we are called not only to act but also to be patient observers. When we do so, we may well discover the laws of liminal domains such as circularity.

If the coastline is the place where the sea and land meet, and the brain is where the mind meets matter, then what happens when the instrument of consciousness, the brain, shifts and changes? Surely, throughout life the body remains plastic and responsive to every experience. Neuroscientists have proven that repeated experience, whether it be that of the cabdriver, violinist, or meditator, changes the brain itself. Yet what if the change is driven no longer by outer experience or mental gymnastics? What if, instead, the brain changes are pathological? What changes in the lived experience of one with Parkinson's or Lewy bodies? For people like Alexander and me the solid grounding offered by outer experience may be weakened so that the mind is less tightly tethered to the sense world.

What are we to make of visions and hallucinations? Can experience ever lie? Experience is the given, the starting point of conscious life. What did Goethe mean when he remarked that there was no such thing as a visual illusion, declaring instead, "visual illusion is visual truth"? We can delight in the innocent tricks of perspective, colored shadows, and other so-called optical illusions. We are drawn in and laugh, curious as to how the mind can be so clever and yet so mistaken. If engaged properly, every visual illusion has the potential to open up one or another of the mind's secrets. Far more has been learned about color vision from color blindness than in any other way. Every deficit, every defect is a natural experiment from which we can learn a great deal. What can we learn about the mind, about poetry, about life from those with Parkinson's, Lewy bodies, or other neurological disorders? Here is a start.

Two parts are required for meaningful experience. By that I mean that percept and concept must be joined if the buzzing, blooming confusion of raw sense input is to become meaningful. Veridical knowledge results when percept and concept are congruent, well-matched. The union of percept and concept goes along largely unconsciously, thank God. What a burden it would be to make every connection between the two consciously. The struggle to see, to make meaning through vision has been researched on those recovering from congenital blindness. The challenges are huge and largely unsuccessful. Somehow in childhood each of us learns to see, to hear, and to make meaning of what we see and hear. I view this as part of the grace given to children in the first three years, parallel to learning how to walk and speak. The rich full world of the senses becomes for us a language, dense with meaning and significance. What was given in childhood is taken from us all too frequently in old age: memory, meaning, and clear sight all diminish.

Yet Alexander shows us in both his poems and his essay,

"My Life with Lewy," that old age not only takes away, but also gives. It can grant us an un-asked-for liberation from a mentality that is perhaps too rigidly literal, too well-grounded. If we can retain sufficient self-awareness, then the surprises and ambiguities of a shifting consciousness can become our friend, leading us to unfamiliar but remarkable corners of consciousness.

❧

Suppose that associating a concept with a percept was not so reliable—it never is perfectly so for any of us. Suppose it was a varied and dynamic process such that rather frequently a tree limb was seen as an outstretched arm, or a boulder was a pair of wrestling bearded old men, or the shadows beneath the apple tree seemed to hide furtive figures. Can we imagine what new stories or mythologies might arise in the wake of such awareness? Maybe we need to practice hallucinating more, but in a manner that preserves a deep stillness, a centered surety not grounded in matter but in mind or spirit. It would be a type of awareness that would permit us to navigate in a domain of experience that would otherwise remain uncharted and even frightening.

I think that the courageous neurologist and writer Oliver Sacks experimented over many years with hallucinogens for this reason. In meditation, likewise, one must learn increasingly to do without familiar landmarks. Rudolf Steiner describes how for imaginative cognition images free themselves from bodies, becoming for all intents and purposes like hallucination. If, however, we can find a new and living ground for our thinking, then new concepts will light up in us, and new and living thinking dawns within us.

As we live longer and longer, the experience of dementia becomes more common, becoming even an expected part of the passage from this world of sense certainties to the spirit world of suprasensible reality. Who knows, perhaps that period in our lives when so much is lost can be thought of as a practice time for the beyond. Surely we should and do treasure our sanity, but can we not, even here, at the threshold of loss, find a silver lining in the cloud of unknowing?

Having lived so long in the same community, Alexander and I have shared the loss to death of friends and family members. It is appropriate at our age to look back on those we have loved but who are gone, and to ponder mortality, to think about what death might be for us. Can we even now begin to trace out its shoreline? Can we learn to navigate its boundaries and thresholds ahead of time? In accompanying those we love to the threshold of death, and loving them still beyond death, we are in a sense practicing dying by means of empathy. When recently asked concerning his own meditative life, the Dalai Lama replied that he was practicing for his death.

Thoreau tells us that he went to the woods to "live deliberately" such that when he came to die he would not discover that he had not lived. In old age the converse may well be true also. We should die with a certain deliberateness, with a consciousness of the threshold crossing and its stages. We will be grateful for its blessings, recalling the friendships we have had, the love given and received, realizing that we have lived fully and well.

In the final poem of the collection, Alexander writes of Spring:

> I would be ambushed by the budding
> as I listened through the window,
> and I would taste at last the sap
> of how the music happens.

He listens through the window. Once again, he is separated, this time from the budding of the blossoms and the flowing of the sap, by a boundary of hard clear glass as tough to cross as brain or barbed wire. But, Alexander instructs us, if you look you will notice a messenger standing at the fiery open threshold wearing a dusty old hat. She will welcome you in with song. No one else can see her; she is there for you alone. Sing your way across the barrier; that is how the music happens.

ARTHUR ZAJONC is former President of the Mind & Life Institute and Emeritus Professor of Physics at Amherst College, where he taught from 1978 to 2012.

THE BRAIN IS A BOUNDARY

THE BRAIN IS A BOUNDARY

The brain is a boundary.
On this side: glucose, hemoglobin, dopamine.
On the other: untamed lightness
of elephants treading the spirit savanna,

a parade of prophets on shining unicycles,
sackfuls of song slung over their shoulders,
saints cascading over a cragged rock face
into a lagoon fed by the spring of glimpses.

On that side, even the mosses speak clear
philosophy. A snowy egret stands alone,
open-eyed, her beak agape to the sun.
The border, like barbed wire, gives warning

of the sting attending unauthorized crossings,
but also weakens and crumbles with age,
allowing small ones to pass through unnoticed.

KEEP THE PENCIL SHARP, ALWAYS MOVING

Keep the pencil sharp, always moving.
That was one of the instructions
I tried to remember.

Most had dissolved
when I woke up wet, tangled in vines
under the tree.

Just these two:

1.
Be certain about your awareness
of the curtain separating
the roof of truth

from the dentils
or metaphysical tailings
adhering there, biting.

2.
Welcome, embrace
the willow's dance, lonely,
for you almost only.

FLOSSING MY MIND

Flossing my mind, a word
came out, fell to the floor,
and with a barely audible
–ping–
bounced up to land dead
at the side of the sink
in a pulsating splatter of
reddish pink at the edge,
evidence of recent life,
more recent dying.

So sad, and yet,
in the painful words
of another stock phrase,

dead words happen

It's why we can't think.

Indeed they die so young,
so attentively ignored,
that we take little notice
even as their solidified corpses
are paraded up and down,
as if by sleight of hand they'd re-inhabit
the word-souls long since departed
to their moist and shadowy reward.

This one was different.
I saw it die, I felt it struggle
for that moment like a fledgling
just about to fly, before my
mindless efforts plucked it
from a thicket of supra-cranial energies,
ripped its nascent self out of
the womb of words, ejected it
into this, our cold, clean, analytic world,
where the flag of stone and gravity
stands unfurled, a realm where
translucent word-flesh
cannot for more than moments
stay meaningfully alive.

But I did notice this time
And cradled its corpse
with a new reverence.

BELIEVE IN THE SILVER EGRET

Try to believe in the silver egret
resting in still blue water.

If you escape the shackles of time
you will come to know that behind her eyes

is an impossibly high mountain
layered over with sheets of gold.

Give of your all to her,
unwittingly, without concern.

She will be neither embarrassed
nor embraced by your attention.

At length will you sense the wind
as it brings in a great four-masted schooner,

sails covering all the sky,
their fabric drawn taut with purpose.

You will be startled by thunder cracking behind,
bolts of lightning tearing the sky ahead,

and, you may notice smaller white birds fluttering over foam.
At this moment, above all,

believe in the silver egret
resting in still blue water.

KNOWING

I know there is liquid in my spine,
though I can't exactly feel it.
I know blood is born
deep in my marrow,
though I seem asleep to it.
I even sense the wormlike
little packages,
who, from each cell's core, control
my every move, my sighs and
inspirations.

But just as a purple chicory
blooms on the rotted bed
of a Model A rusting in old woods,
I have another sense emerging.
It gives me the feel of being liquid–like.
The forms of water inform this knowing.
I spiral around a dim idea,
invite its borders to get in the way of me,
allow my flowsense to vortex, meander
round about it,
eddying, whirling:
like the snail shell in my hand,
a spiral encounter
leading to something
that might outlast water.

THE UNLIKELIHOOD OF BEING

THE UNLIKELIHOOD OF BEING

A fleeting, orgasmic interlude
on a warm, hard chair. I was
aroused by purest probability,
by raw, whole numbers
dribbling off my lips
onto the glowing legs,
waiting below like overfed
parentheses.

Pulsing helplessly,
driven by primitive multiplicative lust,
wet, hot, red, wildly
sliding down a bell-shaped curve,
I came
to be a statistic.

STONE CIRCLES

Of all the rounded, sea-thrown stones
on my grandfather's beach,
some were stolid, clunky, future doorstops
who tended to keep their positions
a safe distance from the water's usual edge.
Closer to that verge of ocean
You could find the more active ones,
fist-sized or smaller,
moving in a tidal dance
of daily perpetual commotion,
following cues from moon and sea.
A certain few of these stones had rings;
magic rings, I knew, with
colored belts, circles, speckles,
mapmakers' markings of eccentric worlds,
not nearly spherical but hand perfect.

If you can catch one of these
stones, grip it fast in both hands
so as to squeeze out all your brainish thoughts
and summon up a wish that's been
waiting in the root cellar, getting sadly limp
with carrots in a box of sealess sand.
Then, holding wish and stone together
in your stronger arm, throw them both
in a slowly arcing curve into the sea.

You will get your wish, bearing
truth enough to feed you lunch.
It works because the stone circle
was born from the sky,
precipitated out of planetary paths
onto this very stone,
finished and delivered to your hand
by the motion of the alchemical salt waters.

However,
you must be sure to throw
further than the low tide mark,
beyond where pink granite disrobes,
exposing its private seaweed wetness to all.
If you don't throw far enough,
you won't get your wish
but you'll get your stone again.
And you might not know
that it's been waiting, maybe for
years, crawling back to you,
compelled by its own wish for circularity
to look you in the eye again.

LIMA BEAN GIRL

She was a lima bean girl.
I was a gray-flannel suited six year old boy.
Her face waxy, plump, beanish,
my suit scratchy, strange,
a spectacular shell.
I had a shoebox with hearts on it,
a slit on top to let valentines in.
Walking home I found a turtle
in the stone wall near the Raushenbush's house.
He lived happily in the valentine box
because the slit let air in.
Lima bean girl had narrow slits for eyes,
so I couldn't quite see everything.
The turtle had wise wide eyelids.
She was my lima bean valentine
but the turtle lived closer to my heart.

ME NOT IN THE PHOTOGRAPH

That's not my face in the photograph.
It never is my face in the photograph.
It's not me in the negative,
not in the black, not in the white,
not behind the gray of mittens
in the lower right corner.
I'm not under the blue wool cap or
under the fear on that face or anywhere
near my father's angry, bald head,
redness spreading over it but
not visible in the old black and white
photograph that has neither color nor truth.

If you squint, peering as you would
to notice a goldfinch in the forsythia;
if you stop looking for my face where
it is not and will never be, then you might
imagine your way into the stucco house
behind the children with the man
and the woman—sun and moon
in quaking collision—and you could go
up all the stairs and through a door into
an attic room of chests and hanging shapes
and you will find there a small chest,
painted white with three drawers, each with
a place cut out in the front so you can pull
it, but when you pull they squeal as if
to say the drawer is not forbidden exactly

but at the edges of some other world
you'll never find in photographs.

Maybe you won't believe me, but I'm telling
you that my face, the one not in the photograph,
is not behind the mittens, not anywhere out there.
It is in the middle drawer.
But by now it might have become a butterfly,
long gone.

FIRST TIME

The first time
there was enough time;

time to notice creases on cherries,

time for you to miss a train
and stand dumb in the hissing
steams and squeals of Victoria Station;

time for left luggage
to be left to itself.

Enough time for the ripples
on old green window panes
to mirror truly our first waters,
the new dew of who to you.

Time for eyes, for the yes in eyes.

Huddled on the floor
we found time even for a taste
surpassing cherries.

WILD ROSES

For example,
in the beginning was a rose,
actually a handful of roses,
wild, thorny unkempt pinkshot
gathered at the meadow's edge
where the land sometimes forgets itself
and schismatized, slides seaward.

Later I was sitting safely on the warm, green, summer ground,
my shoulder blades looking past either side of the silver birch
that kept my sitting upright.
All around were dense, skying waters, unmoved as yet.
In my lap, looking right into my eyes,
or perhaps at the still leaves above,
was your face, framed by meandering hairstreams,
touched by a smile that came and went
as lightly as caressing air
that aroused small hushed voices from the birch.

And the rose—all right, the roses, many roses.
I'm still afraid it might have been excess,
an unhealthy dose,
like too much rain too soon.
But, at the time, it seemed
to be within the right ratio,
in accord with how things were settling into place,
becoming what they were.
Yes, the wild roses.

AFTER THE ONIONS

Join me, you, after the onions.
We, peeling till weeping,
speak, eyes glisten,
shot through with vegetable vapors.
You glance soft across the broad oak table,
five hours to go until giving thanks.

Now, we prepare the carcass, insult it
with celery, salt, basil, bread, oregano,
and the onions. I notice onion bits clinging
to the knife edge. On the back of a spoon
I catch the image of delectable you
invading a yam, one shoulder raised
as your head leans to it, looks my way.

Then into the heat of an oven,
and out we two
in silence go, lie down
beyond the barn, pressing
long, old grass of November,
pale yellow as peels,
into hardening ground
that will surely remember
she of the oniony hair and moist brown
eyes, swallowing the falling yellow
of a short day's light in afternoon, and he, I,
eager to place his life in the bowl of her spoon,
come taste what may.

IF I OPEN WIDE ENOUGH

If I open wide enough
I cry, from too much light, I guess,
illuminating more of this world
than a person can ever understand.

So I try to ignore certain things:
the persistent efforts of earthworms
and how many waves crash with
no one listening, and each of

the moon's faces and where exactly
she walks. But when I happen upon
a single moment of pure budding,
or you, peaceful, with your chin

upon the left hand bent,
my censorship fails and I am in
the big it again, celebrating
just to contain my heartbreak.

AFTER SUNDAY MORNING LOVE

A fly gallops across the room,
buzzing louder than air, hovers now
above the canyons where we in cool sheets
float after Sunday morning love.

Drawn from somewhere not else
into my senses again, I wander
with the footstep of your eyelid,
opening, open, open, close,

opening, open, open, close,
and feel the tidal rush of air
in and out of your lips, breaking
on my eyebrow's coast, traces

of some new notion scudding by.
The song of your skin resting
along mine is a familiar circle,
like the chanting of hymns down

the road at the other communion.
The fly gossips, and no annoyance,
only slow whispers of breath
rise inward between us.

MOMENT ON THE SOFA

Listen, if I could peel
the leather from my face,
then you might see the rippled
sacramental sands lying hopeful
under Cassiopeia; there, at the
terrifying edge where salt water
washes over the quivering
instant of pink, granite flesh.

You might hear the murmur of dune
grasses nipping at your feet, sharp
into your soles, inviting attention
towards what lives beneath, bellowing
for your ear, your wonder, thirsting
for the wetness of you.

You would see the ends of all roads
joining where a red cow grazes,
her bag achingly full. You would see
the wrinkled girl wandering there,
moonlight fillowing off her shoulders
as she places her pulse in waves
alive with mackerels and electricity.

Behind my face I could also
take you to see the man with the thick fur
hat who lives in the far north with
wolves, his pine hut abandoned

to ice. On the rough table with one
leg missing sit your letters unopened,
unread. In the corner is the unfed
fire, now just a faint, gasping glow.

But listen, my face is as it is,
and you must settle for this
moment on the sofa, our
fingers touching, when
all I seem to do is glance
somewhat in your direction
with eyebrows raised.

THIS IS AWKWARD

This is awkward, so don't stop me
if I meander or sometimes swallow
my words into my chest, where
they splinter into sound shards slicing
through cartilage and bone, causing
my breath to have unnatural rhythms.

I will sip tea from a glass and take
a shortbread from the basket
on the kitchen table. I will sigh again
and again, and again I will sigh.
Seeing the fear on your forehead
and at the sides of your mouth, I
will want to speak of how the leaves
on the maple tree at the north end
of the pasture are turning already.

It's so soon, surprising everyone,
so unexpected, like a heavy first
snow laid down during sleep, or
like just these days now, when all
you can do is hope that we will discover
a forgotten text that speaks rightly
of the dance we've landed in.

Surprising, and yet somehow
familiar, like open lips
when you just can't find the words
to clothe sorrow.

WHOLE MOON STORY

In the mirror of your arm
over mine, I see the whole
moon story, the horses

galloping, the hot wind.
I see why you stayed even
when the dance seemed over,

musicians drifting away,
turning off lights, closing
doors. You stayed even then

because of a moon and long
grasses around a pool, blessing
us deeper than we knew.

BRING ME ALONG

Bring me along when you leave your body,
even if it's in wet, grey snow, amid confusion
next to the car.
Or holding an apple
near the bottom of the tall wooden ladder
leaning among high twigs that brushed your cheeks
in the ancient apple tree across the unkempt field,
that had been a pasture once
and would again rejoice at being
cut, trimmed, bitten, well-manured,
lived in on purpose.

When you decide to leave,
or even if you prefer to stay—but can't—
as apples would keep hanging forever in the sun,
but in one chosen instant drop
down to ground as offering to the future;

Let me be there

to pick up that ripeness
and bring it with care inside the house,
so you might walk gently with footsteps
out of these days and nights
feeling a warm hand touching
just your cheek a bit without you,
knowing that my whispers, whys and laughs
and awkward worldless moments, and tears,

do behold of who you are, now.
Our love, even when you've gone,
is as real of you as redness is of apples
after they are only a remembered sweetness
on the tongue, or lying in the snow.

DREAM OF MINE

It's cold outside.
Inside, my bones rattle and shake
because nothing else is to be done.

Cold.
Pigeons complain,
breathing their bobbing breaths,
filling their insides with sooty
airborne messages from

someone's brass-framed
drawing room fireplace,
a polished marble mantel bearing relief
sculptures of creatures, ladies, gods

or what? One is not
after all, meant to linger
on fireplace decorations
to the point of recognition.

Cold.
And my hands chew one another,
grasping their favorite food,
familiar flesh, squeezing
a random finger or a well known fold
so hard that I remember where I am and
why the woman with the white pasty face,
white legs and shoes, brought me here

to this cold and empty outside inside place
where this one can't remember
why anything is.

In my pocket is the book of poems
and I need to blow my nose;
Where in this place
could there ever be a cloth handkerchief?
Men opened the black trunk that had been

in dreams of mine. They
unfolded cloths, canvasses bearing
other dreams, as one of the
white-shoed women mounted
a black wooden chair,
hammered
a nail into the wall, hung
the cloth so you could see
the whole happening dream.

My arms ache.
I think I might be sad.

THE FALL

Why did it come to be
that one of the seasons—those four
cleanly cut quarters that herd us onward
along the annual parade route

(forced march) of temporality—why
is one given the most awful designation
of all, namely,
Fall?

What are these tilt-induced seasons for?
They lean us into the possibilities
of renewal, death, and a new view,
an image-rich narrative seeking to incarnate

the astro-solar journey of circular return above
into our mystified lives, looking for love below.
The four stand along the parade
route, trumpets sounding forth their fanfare

at the curb, while we sheepishly believe we're here
to be protected as we meet the verdict of
this latest Fall that backwardly refers to a primeval
error that now repeats and reoccurs,

with guilty knowledge in each leaf-like fall
into the sin of Being alone in this earth's
body we reside us in. I cannot but uplook
wondering, if this spice of life's so pungent

that we must fall again to crawl,
breathing to keep alive the sweet aroma
of the humus that will, with softening embrace
receive us in, as unguent for

death's arrival, with a certain coolness
at the door, and sharp precision in the knock.

PHOTOGRAPH OF MOTHER AT
THANKSGIVING

In this one you are opening
the oven, wide-eyed in hot
wind of turkey, knowing only
this: your memory of how to
cook this bird has slipped
into low tide waters where
it will sink still deeper.

On this day of gratitude
none is offered for a brain
that, like a candle, disappears
even as its flame glows,
visible in eclipse.

As you open the stove door
your face flutters with traces
of something about how long
meat cooks, about squirting liquids,
a possibility of peas, perhaps
something red,
a fog of berries.

On your face is
a lengthening moment
of catching up with something
moving slowly, black
and white cows in a field,

drifting across at dusk
into another place
I cannot yet see.

AT LUNCH

How do you measure forgetting?
How do you find your way through
the endless folding labyrinth of an old brain
that has gradually become like a dry sponge,

intricately textured but holding
not a drop of clear water?
You might reach across the table
to remind your mother what a spoon is for,

and still remember that we bear within us
not only brains but beating, blood-filled hearts
that have thoughts as well, not so solid
as spoons but far more open and more full.

Heart's thoughts can reach back across a table
and grab you while you're counting time or money
or her spoonfuls of soup, and let you know that
even a mother with a sleeping brain does not forget you.

WHETHER YOU CAN HEAR ME

I do not know whether you can hear me
or not. The words, I mean, my whispering
into the palm of your hand, the words

I form carefully with tongue, lips, teeth,
and the other mysterious mouthparts,
as breath rises from behind, it seems,

on its own wisdom-driven rhythm.
The words, "alright," "butterfly," "don't know," "time,"
each one a stairway ascending to an open window,

the curtains pulled aside and tied, but
fluttering in the wind of this hand-made moment.
The words, like the granules of rich soil,

have ample space between each place
where an admixture of fear, love, and is-ness
resides, where living, speaking softly, and dying

are woven into the listening of the other.
Words like "alright," "body," or just, "goodbye."
Sometimes, when breath comes to rest, words

keep moving across the room, through the door,
up the stairs, out the window, to be caught up
in the songs of lilacs or blackbirds, to be

seduced by the unbearable call of this
rising now with you moon,
with words like, "maybe."

MOTHER PASSING ON THE SOLSTICE

Death, like a solstice, slinks
to a soul-specific, chosen eyeblink
that, legal and clockwise, officially occurs: doctor
certified, penned, kenned and kerned on granite,
socked on a slab of fallen grout for good, or forgot.

Birth, our first passing, is so slippery that,
at once, it slides into an eddy of "can't recall."
Of dying our knowledge is secondhand
if it is anything at all. And so I speculate
and try to snag a taste of how the going feels.

I sense less the gripping, viselike
compression that can settle
into deepwater murk, where sediment
nearly obscures the second-hand
forced-marching to its inescapable end.

No, a different mood lurks here, its aroma everywhere around,
with a persistent drone, a searing, threshing sound,
a being whose form is hugely splayed, an inside-outness thrown
about by gusts, exposing molteness of guts
a glacier, slow rolling in its crushing advent, grinding

whatever mortal dares to wrestle
in that grimstone wake place where grief
comes hollering in the only second left after the one
when there lay a person still, now just a body,
(unjust to call her "just" a body), her countenance

recounting all that's been inhabiting those hands
eyes, mouth, ears and every holy or official hole
whose vapors brought me into birth through
the inland waterway of both forgetting
and begetting.

In lush fog she leaves shore on lingering breath.

Eons since the dying began to not be going, her
body is left to itself. Released from the grip of time,
she displays the presence in every sinew of someone's mother,

mine, doing her best to do it right, leaving
footprints in gray sands at dead low tide.

THE DEAD ARE NOT DEAD

—After Birago Diop

The dead are not dead.
It is we the living who are dead,
to think they are.

A moment after my mother's
last small breath, her whole face
puckered tightly as if she was
squeezing something out,

and then relaxed completely.

We all looked at one another, speechless,
eyes wide with wonder, wet with love.
I firmly patted her almost fleshless leg
and said, "Well done!" I meant to praise
her dying.

Later, after some tea, we carried her
body into the bedroom, where
she would stay for several days,
to let her leave in peace, among friends
without interference. We were lucky
she had chosen winter.

It was late morning, a few hours after
the solstice, as the sun slowly emerged
from behind heavy gray clouds. I stared

into her face. The Alzheimer's that she had
borne with such amazing grace, with smiles

and childlike delight, was suddenly, entirely
gone. Looking at this now regal countenance,
I realized for the first time, and with some
astonishment,
who she is.

AT THE MEMORIAL GATHERING

Do I try now to recall a memory, say,
of walking with my mother on a new mown path,
then through swaying summer grass to the beach below,
where her good friends, sand dollar and sea urchin

found their way into her delighting hands.
Loutish sea gulls scattering from the dock as
my father marched resolute toward the sea,
halting for a moment to look back and say,

with affectionate irritation "Let's go, sweetie."
He moved ahead in his still determined stride,
while she lagged behind where water, earth, and air
commingled with the dwindling light.

She wondered aloud what it might be like to be a snail, or
to occupy galactic forms beyond the sky,
and whether deer could sense us in this moment
from their hiding place in a copse close by.

After breathing in the salty air enlivened by
breaking waves and the fragrance of tall
evergreens, she asked me a not quite
unexpected question, something like

how did I like being me,
and other queries looking for a deeper
introspective vein. Then as she
crunchwalked across the beach

now with seaweed in her pocket and
the sky running to her eyes,
I could feel the air was shifting
from breeze to friendly wind,

and saw that he had gone ahead.
It was time for him to be sailing, to
surrender to what wind and water
offered at this time and place of passage.

Now the tide was low, sun setting in rosy purples,
music of ocean and sky embroidering her form
as she glided gently over the dock, so quietly
that even gulls stayed to witness her passage.

CARROTS

When I am dead, planted below crumbly humus,
I shall keep watch for carrots moving past
on their journey to the center of the universe.
I may wait long, as when a bus is terrible late
coming, but when those orange sunshot arrows
pierce through my horizon or my pelvis
I'll snatch them—and be finally at peace,
fingering roots.

ORANGE ANSWER

If I was the orange brilliance in the leaving trees
across the still green pasture,
I would finally have my answer
for this moment,
and as easily as I'd slide my withering sole
out of an old, leather boot,
I'd release that color,
and know within my own drying veins
that seasons shift as sure as socks and shoes do,
and why not reasons, too?

I meet orange, strangely, everywhere today.
I can neither touch its inward pulse
nor whistle quite how questionly
it whys and waves into my steady-seaming floorboards,
leaving me full flat without foundation or solidity.

VISIT FROM HENRY

I was in the red armchair, by the fire,
when Henry came rushing in, grinning.
He seemed to sing these words:
>   I have learned the language of the Dead. Amen!
>   I have learned the language of the Living. Amen!
Only these words.
He perspired heavily—unusual for the dead—
but then I saw he was drenched
in the delight of his discovery.

I didn't know if I could believe him,
whether he was real—
not "real" like the armchair,
but real like words skimming through air
in the wake of a grasshopper's flying
or love across borders
or longing.
Solid in my wondering I reached
for my tea and he was gone.

WHO IS DELIVERED

Who is delivered, tall in khadi cloth
across the threshold of international arrivals
in the glare of airport glitz and shining
coffee cheer? Who arrives to me at last
after so many others' arms and legs glide in
over fresh waxed linoleum tiles,
each nine inch tile—like each star—for
some one body? Who in this river
arrives after so many streaming faces
that are wrong to me, passing curiosities
in odd clothing, bodies whose aroma I do not
recognize? I am not tied to them.
They will not pluck me as I will be
plucked when my son arrives to me.
Who arrives? Who is delivered
to me?

The woman with too red lips wilts
in her sari, follows ten paces behind
her bulbous faced man. She does not breathe
the confidence wafting off the folds
of his important trench coat. This woman
does not matter to me; as I laugh at her
I hear the escalator teeth scraping
at my cruelty. She is not delivered
to me.

I am weak with the waiting
for these faces to be delivered

and to grow away from here, as foam
on the tide that brings my son homing
from the other side of earth,
from Bodh Gaya, from Bihar, from Orissa,
from Dehra Dun, from other worlds.
But as the tide recedes and at last
I see he is not dead or lost or arrested or
injured or bleeding or on wheels or gone,
I am seized by the panic of knowing
that I do not know
who is arriving here.
Surely the eighteen year old boy
who slipped through these glass walls
and left the earth here one year ago
cannot inhabit the tall body in khadi
walking from Flight 36, Delhi to Boston, walking
now through international arrivals
on worn rubber flip-flops.

He tells of the theft of his camera,
his photographs, his tape recorder,
and his books. Who is delivered to me
carries a sitar, a violin, some few clothes, a flute.
He tells how he had to lose the practical things
to discover the beautiful ones which then revealed
themselves to be more truly practical.
He says that is India.

This is my arrival,
who is delivered to me.

LET THERE BE WAR

Let there be war.
We declare it.
And a sky, not
a heaven, with
startling blues,
B-52's
meaningless news.

All these we declare.

Let there be a naming
of who is evil and who is not,
and a calculating
of how many corpses,
and how many reasons
for what we declare.

Let the dead ones
be healed of their high surprise,
that when they speak to us
we may be washed,
our moments of silence joining together
into an unbroken night sky
whose stars cannot be counted.

Let this be my final declaration.

NEVER TELL ME THAT AGAIN. NEVER.

Never tell me that again. Never.
And when you do, first make sure
you are standing under the black nets

we use to prevent the birds from stealing
every single blueberry. What greed
radiates from their beady eyeballs

as they think of eating the fruits; the fruits
of our unpaid labors. What rapture! But
 you must forget these birds as you stare

upward at the whole of the entirely
wide, night sky, higher even
than your innermost experience of dust;

Dust! the cloud of it busily being nothing
follows us everywhere, burrows into
our finest stockings. Can you hear it, full

of sleep and dreams, becoming an afternoon
shadow? Do you remember? And the small
red broom that followed us around after

we died in the fog. Never tell me again,
but try to remember the dust.

MY HANDS, CLEAN

A spoon
a brass bowl,
a line of smoke diffusing in the sky
as the drone disappears,
long pieces of brilliant, colored cloth,
bright like the eyes were.
Rubber sandals, twice repaired,
a small radio on the shelf next to scissors,
a loom,
one small window high on the wall
over the place where the boy
sat all morning, weaving,
one large opening where half of another wall
was removed by the explosion,
a leg here,
an arm there,
the yogurt he was eating from the bowl
swallowed by the floor,
a fly feasting upon blood,
the boy's future fading in the echo of thunder.
My hands, clean, engaged
in remote control.

LIFE ON THE HILL

IN THE ORCHARD

In the orchard
I ambling am,
though motionless
in the knowing
of this boulder-heavy
physicalism, a thingful
all tipped over,
a bushel of pieces
altogether now
in this enormous waiting
for a rift,
a gift to leave me
better unfettered,
unmanacled, decuffed,
no muzzle or snare,

anticipating
the moment
when
the unfallen
apple of October
encounters
the flaw
of gravity.

EVERY EVERY DAY

Every day, every day,
every day day day,
the shining sun sun sun,
shining sun is ever there,
ever there, ever there it goes again,
and again and again and
now it's nebulae around me,
it is night circling round,
all around above my head
with the stars all much too many,
many eyes looking down,
while I'm asleep, running deep,
every time, it's every time
that I sleep where I know
that the each and every dayness
of the solar repetition
is the doorway to the night.

Oh, the night, singing light
as I breathe all of me outward,
feel the pull of my soul
toward the birthing of sun spaces,
into irresistible places
that invite me with a stare
to fly up in between
each embryonic infant word,
and lose my very smallself
in the circling, wandering light,

whose plans I'll never know
because my dome is much too slow,
like the rocks and the stone
that form the blocks and the bone
of my prison.

THE YOUNGER HEN

The one hen is younger than the others,
smaller too, hiding herself in the corner
her rust-brown feathers sleek

with the shine of youth, her bright youth
not yet fully henned in by what will emerge
when she has rounded the curve of arrival

to fully express that she is completely
hen. Not yet. She remains hovering
in the corner, shy as a periwinkle,

remembering the slowness of stars,
their movement a prayer to time.
Whenever I cradle her in my arms

she is able to hear my heart beating,
its pace sedate compared to hers,
and heavier. She, the younger hen,

is like an airborne feather, not yet
fully alighted into gravity's firm grasp.
Her beak speaks a pristine yellow landscape,

evidence of an inner dignity she bears,
a quality quite unknown to the other hens
who dwell in empty boredom, seeking

relief by endlessly pecking their
"protector," a twice rehabilitated and
once hopeful old rooster who used to strut

proudly about. Now, accustomed
to his insulting maltreatment, he occupies
a random spot amid the dreck and

debris of the henhouse floor,
pretending he has great plans for the future.
He is just an old rooster

who doesn't even tell stories. But she,
the younger hen, has stories yet untold.
Each of her unseen feathers will become

a long story, an epic tale of how all music
came to be, and eggs, and the roundness
of the moon, and of the huckleberry

she will presently peck from the palm of my hand.

AT THE FAR END OF THE FIELD

At the far end of the field where our sheep used to be,
about 10 feet beyond the fence, but parallel to it, is the edge
of the property, is the border, between me and my
neighbor (whose name I keep forgetting), and also

between me and the adjoining town.
My neighbor lives in Pelham, while I reside in
the beautifully named town of, well, Belchertown.
If I were a dog I guess I'd pee along this line,

but because it's a few feet beyond the fence line
I don't even think about it, not for a second or two.

I once knew a woman who got kind of restless,
even cranky whenever she felt she was in some
imperceptible proximity to the edges of things,
even property lines, town borders, and most

remarkably, to inwardly informed places.
For example, she could get all edgy, I guess you'd call it,
by suddenly fearing that someone close or just near to her—
a person, a pet, even her favorite houseplant—would

leave or die or just sit down and cease
attending to her in any way whatsoever. It
was like a circular wall might in a certain moment drop
down from heaven to enclose everyone except her.

I wanted to tell her that all her skittishness
was arbitrary, just where the ink hit the paper,
an invisible line like the ones connecting the points
of Pegasus or any other picture in the night sky.

I wanted to tell her this, and to suggest we
should maybe go for a walk together, she and I,
and hold each other's hands, and look at the
skunk cabbages next to the brook

where the old stone walls were slowly falling down,
and maybe we'd sit down in that old cellar hole
along the overgrown road that disappears into
pine and laurel.

But that was in a different place, another time, and
I said nothing as we safely stayed within our bodies.

THE TRUTH OF RICE

Just before dusk, just before supper,
moon somehow aloft,
I give my truth to six middle-aged hens
and one proud rooster.

My gifts include decaying lettuce, old carrots
limp as the fingers of a fresh corpse,
apple cores on the path to rottenhood,
and rice on the way to slimeville.

I bang the scrap container on the outside
of the six by six foot chicken house
to loosen the sticky basmati grains
that are defying gravity, reluctant to leave

their cozy plastic dwelling. Startled
by the noise, the hens, as if one being, all rise
several inches from the earth as though
a judge had just entered the courtroom.

Seconds later, their fears dispersed,
the hens restore order by resuming
their usual manic scavenging, because,
after all, I am their judge, their God,

their benefactor in whom they have
absolute, unswerving faith. Their trust
in me is unbothered by the annoyance
of logic. Their knowing is via pecking,

not thinking, with their little feathered heads
more in motion than our thoughts ever are.
Watching them tasting, testing, digesting the truth of that
rice, I wonder if their hen thoughts

live in the feathers. One old hen has
lost most of hers, or, I wonder, did she just decide
to release them, knowing that she
had nothing new to say under this April moon.

DUSK IN A SPRING PASTURE

Bells,
metal's sounding matters
in rope-drawn rhythms
from a high hill somewhere
until the toll crawls down
into my sternum's aching echo.

Moaning, bellowing sweetness
of cows lazy
on tongue-torn grass of new May,
their savoring the caress
of wild rosebush
on barn-weary hide.

Surprising fullnesses
of fat moon over
apple tree explosion,
the welcome fire of frog song
reborn so answeringly
to no snow now,
that once more
in the roundness of what matters,
I stand stunned,
unready.

UNDER VENUS

I could stand under Venus
on a clear night like this
and lick your most minute, meandering thought
with the tip of my fresh-scraped tongue,
if only you'd hungering let me.

BY THE POOL ONE JUPITER SHINING EVENING

I love you me and stars above,
your shimmering soul in you, in me.
Who would I be with only love
Walking in freedom, who would I be?

If I could find the glimmer of that
rapturous rupture, the crack where
inner light becomes outer life—or
have I turned it all around? Perhaps

the outer light streams through
some world solar magic
into the shining we be when
we behold and are beheld?

Slowly, my eye's light ascends
the steep, cobbly path all unknowingly
to a silken, perfect surprise: delight alive
in the listening quiver of your own eye,

and all the world's together at last,
not lost but so deliciously found,
amazing grateful hearts so vast,
chanting love's own sound.

Who would I be if I were you
and together we walked in what is true,
knowing what's not
is never the new.

The crack in the wall gives a melting light,
reflecting the tears that give us sight.

By the pool one Jupiter shining evening,
I witnessed the light being born a thousand times,
emerging childlike out of the blue-
yellow wedding of day and miraculous night:

a celebration of birthing, burning illumination,
widening cracks inviting the light
that sails within and without
our one heart's home.

By the pool, enrapt by Jupiter's worldwide embrace,
I drank in the likeness of each
of glistening you, reflected stars in almost still water
of a pool where illusions drown and love bids us enter.

Then, a knock at the door.
Is it you?

Just the wind.

MESSAGE IN THE MAILBOX

In a full-mooned midnight
with slow emotion
I walk on shallow air
down the watery path
to the glinting mailbox.

It resembles an old barn
in miniature,
with gambrel roof, rust, dust,
swallows awaiting, as I am,
a message

that may lie within.
Afterwards, they will fly.
Nearby in the darkness
a dog sighs, opens and closes
his mouth as if deciding

not to speak about
nipping at the heels
of the expected messenger.
Blades of grass sidle together,
whispering with the dew.

I look downward,
my gaze following
the path to the mailbox.
The moon glides
into the maples.

I open the mailbox,
almost expecting to see
little people in overalls
scurrying, pitching hay,
sweating on this balmy evening.

But they would surely be asleep.
The message is always the same—
I read it slowly, three times:
The time for night words has passed.
Listen for the rooster.
Wake yourself, make breakfast.

Returning to the house
I sense the ground hardening,
sunlight overspreading the landscape,
Infusing the surface
with painfully sharp outlines.

The message is gone.
There is only the rooster.

CHRONICLES OF LEWY

Four years ago I was given a diagnosis of Lewy Body Disease, a progressive, degenerative brain disorder that leads to a variety of cognitive symptoms including visual illusions and occasional hallucinations. These and other symptoms are challenging on many fronts; but I have, surprisingly, found them also to be a creative stimulus, enriching both the aliveness and transparency that may be encountered in the liminality of "ordinary life."

CHRONICLES OF LEWY I:

ON A BOUNDARY

On a boundary now, a border.
Inside, we are floating, swim
amongst sacred sights.
Out there they are stuck,
in fluid motion, far-flung
figures, as if photography
had been here in a flash
to fit the frame to the border
of this image I am.

But no. A multitude,
a mickle of uncertainties
is who, what, I know.
Yes, I know I don't know,
but the remainder reminds me
that it too will go,
becoming appearance,
what's left to write,
scuttling about from corner to side,
in the guise of an old, slow cat,
or the child of ten,
standing just by my left shoulder,
a silent illusion, again.

CHRONICLES OF LEWY II:

FEBRUARY TREKS

It must be February.
Once again I follow
an unevenly wandering desire
to walk in Winter's crooked woods,
silence scattered by the crack of brook ice
under the crush of me, the repercussion
of an unrecognized memory
discovered this morning in my left trouser pocket
as I watched marvelous dancers in the willow tree.

Thoughts and visions also inhabit my February treks,
or sometimes sail into periphery's vision
disguised, for example, as a rail thin gentlemen
much taller than I, wearing a dark-colored hat; a post
it turns out, seeking his blessed beam.

How can I answer when you seem to ask me
if it might have been different had I remained
in this world, rendered with you on a bed of pine needles?

By diving, heart-first into the sure touch
of your brown-eyes surrender.

CHRONICLES OF LEWY III:

INITIAL VISIT

Initial visit to UMass Memorial Hospital
Department of Neurology.
Patient #45387.01038

Mr. Alexander Dreier, an
affable, right-handed
gentleman, born 1949,
complains of memory decline,
in fact, one notes a sign
of unusual visions
(art from heaven?)
(escaped alligator?)
mild cognitive blasphemy,
—or just a blast of ME?—

Reader is referred
to that one true note known
for musicALexander
Dreier, an affable right-headed
gentlesoul who—STOP—
leaps from midship
in mid-sentence,
staring starry
into the blue-hued
meander of YOU?
Difficulty finding the word.
Logos goes low,
(just sayin' sane).

In UMASS-HOLE MEMORIAL
became lost leader
in oracle space of Corridor 5
for unknown reasons
with diffuse snowing
in posterior region where
manifest crabnormalities detectible,
including threefold ducksology
of Lewy according to
this gentlemaniacal individual
firmamentally insistent that
only the sky is his one true brain.

CHRONICLES OF LEWY IV:

WHAT HAPPENED

I went to an island,
discovered that who I am is where I land,
all is island.

This island, named Vinalhaven,
sits 16 miles out to sea
from the Maine land, sustained
by lobstering and visitors (as
this one) who have fallen in love.

Where do I begin?

In beginning is the
forested moss green
glowing glaze where mist,
fog and granite meet
earth, water, air and heat.

When you are there
you are who you are there,
and where dwells the rest
of you may not be known.
I was in a cabin at the base

of towering (150') Starboard Rock,
no locks or email,
only my clattering thoughts

and, increasingly, the artistry
of Lewy distracting me

as I floated mist-filled into
countless crevices of
this boulder-strewn wonder
reaching into sky,
accompanied by the wise squawking

of ravens and the more transporting,
soulful tones of a rarely visible hermit thrush.

I was here to write, I thought, but
as I deepened my engagement
with this ethereal forest in the days
leading up to the full moon, I felt instead
the powerful presence of such rich
beingness, that thoughts lost

their ordinary contours, as rock
became entire soft moss,
my eye's friend and true earth
companion. The forest shyly
revealed her many faces as if gesturing

to the uncertainty in my widening sight,
and my astonishment when a group
of leaf-bedecked indigenous children
emerged from the surrounding fringes,
reaching out askingly until I invited them in.

But what of their parents? Such queries
evoked only a wordless quietude

from these voiceless beings, conundrums
beating from another dimension as inaccessible as
the encircling clouds of fog. Several adults

eventually appeared inside my car, parked
where I'd left it earlier. From a short distance
they resembled average, everyday people,
but when I approached and opened the car door
the seven occupants evaporated altogether

in an instant, leaving not the slightest trace behind.
Soon others arrived, how or from where I had
no idea though I later noticed their ability
to pass through walls with evident ease.
Eventually, some fifteen to twenty people had

assembled in the small cabin, all of them
apparent participants in some mystical process
of shamanic self-discovery, many having
brought magical arts or technologies,
all voiceless, tireless, and requiring no food or water.

My own presence in this peculiar gathering
had come about seemingly by accident as I was
unknown to them and they to me. My knowledge
of their intentions came only through inference as

they relentlessly refrained from speaking. Indeed,
it was I who finally violated this rule
as the night grew longer and my patience with their
behavior eroded. I announced that I had to speak,
that I needed to tell them who I was

as well as to learn who they were and what
they were doing in a cabin they neither owned
nor rented and why they persisted in this obstinate
refusal to communicate, (though I did wonder
if telepathy, real or imagined, might be the answer).

I soon realized that although they heard my words
they would not respond. I indicated that this gave
me no alternative but to call for conventional help
by contacting the island police. I further informed
them that I bore them no ill will but wanted them

to know that they appeared to be violating a wide
variety of laws which could lead to fairly dire
consequences for them. At this point there was a change
in their demeanor as they considered (I supposed)
the importance of what I had just said.

Remaining speechless, they scattered into the woods
both to escape and to activate a number of quite
amazing technologies and visual tricks;
becoming invisible at will, causing trees
to spin around in place, to walk around

and to emit showers of sparks, to name a few.
Interestingly, while they remained speechless
during this time, many of them made unusually
realistic animal-like noises that seemed designed
to scare off me or the police or anyone outside the group.

By the time the patrol car arrived only a few
of the people remained in or around the house. A few
of the technologies were still in use but the officer

seemed remarkably unobservant or uninterested,
preferring to conclude that nothing seemed "amiss."

After speaking by phone with my wife who was
due to arrive by ferry the next morning, I felt it prudent
to allow the officer a few words with her as well. All
three of us were in agreement that it would be unwise
for me to spend another night alone in the cabin.

I soon reached friends living on the island
who kindly offered me a sofa to sleep on
after the officer drove me to their house.
In the morning, my wife arrived, accompanied by her brother,
a psychiatrist.

After hearing my story,
he characterized the experience as "a psychotic episode;"
my wife suggested "a waking dream."

Author's Note: Rule out possible fairy possession.

CHRONICLES OF LEWY V:

THE MILL PRIVILEGE

Borne by a notion delivered amidst
spruce-winds of unrivaled tallness,
whipping their abruptly sharp aroma
in multiple directions, I find myself

seated on the wide expanse of a
broad, sloping slab of granite
that seems to slide into the naked
mudflats of pure, dead low tide.

Rocks of all shapes, sizes, textures,
are strewn across the oozy sludge
floor. Most are granitic, many have
almost geometric forms with

relatively few planar surfaces. Some
appear to be emerging with intent
from the mud that grips them, or the
sharp barnacles forever stuck fast.

Midday. I feel a pleasant heat
rising from the sun-soaked rock,
warming my thighs and back as
I meet this small corner cove

belonging to a tidal inlet known
as the Mill Privilege. Today, though one

sees no sign of mills, I feel the grind
of grand encircling movements in close waters,

and in the push and pull and push
exerted from the sun and moon, and forces from afar,

in slowly stirring trees, as dead low flow proceeds
into a weakened trickle, near death in deed.

Then. The most imperceptibly precise
instant in this dance figure occurs as
two worlds exchange hands, glances, places.

Ebb becomes flow—
Flow becomes ebb.
systole and diastole
meet once again.

I came here alone, but as the tidal exchange
happens, so also do my perceptive
faculties alter, revealing dozens, even
hundreds of sculpted or drawn figures,
each with its own characteristic expression.

Directly across the cove from me is
 a curved row of huge heads gazing
upwards from their mud home, or in some
cases, straining to converse with another.

Nearby is a more or less flat frieze
with a family of nine large, flat figures
including several toddlers and two ancient
elders, all posing as if for a daguerreotype.

Elsewhere, facing into a corner formed by two huge
blocks is a three-dimensional, stone herring gull,
of ordinary size, in beak to beak gull colloquy
with another large bird I am unable to identify.

Also in the cove is a granite sheep, a pig, and,
a little further away on a gravelly rise,
a group of stone creatures resembling
hippos, cows, and other ungulates.

The trees are laden with lichen,
their animated dance forms
weaving bearded mythic figures
into dramatic presentations,

of fairy kings and queens
assisted by antelopes and an amorous
 couple rolling about in the mud

More disturbing is the elephantine creature
who enthusiastically eats the abdomen of an
elegant, mustachioed gentleman,
sporting a carefully coiffed seaweed hairdo.

His gruesome demise is halted by the sound of a car
coming down the drive. My wife must be back from
her errands. I recall my promise to stack the wood.

CHRONICLES OF LEWY VI:

FORTUNATE I AM

Fortunate I am
to inhabit this moment
on the beach,
touching
vacated snail shells,
devoid of life,
yet inhabited
by her spirals,
bathed in the tide
of the Who
that was here.

Fortunate I am
to enter
this world as a rosy hand
enters a glove for protection
from the icy stillness of dust,
still able to touch, to feel
the mother material of earth life
without being singed
by the raw heat
of being.

Fortunate I am
to wear this glove,
this five-fingered body
that touches the world, tells me

what is so fiercely inside
while shielding my heart
from too much terror, or wonder.
This ancient hand that grasps the knob,
knows this door is for opening and closing,
for finding the surprise of You here,
in this world touching.

Fortunate it is to be touched.

THRESHOLDS

I AM OF THE SKY

I am of the sky,
of that sky reflected
here in my flatful palm.

My longing to return
to my home—sky there
is written in the iris blue

infusion that bowls me
in an instant through
my chicory true,

here in the feathered folds
of extra-cranial déjà vu,
departure is fed by a breeze

as I sit with children eating
crackers, I do, discovering
my lover in the dome over you

above all, empty-handed
of what we once knew,
hearts trembling,

wondering, if not us, then who?

THE MESSENGER

Who but the last cloud
knows what this isthmus is,
not narrow mined but ground,
down where arrival is departure,

where contrails of sweat-soaked
expectations slip into streaming
blue lightness? Who do eyes see
without the cartload of luggage we

gathered up before words,
when I first noticed you at the
fiery open threshold, wearing
that old dusty hat of the universe?

You were arresting, radiant palms,
facing the midheaven, where
the cusp was in big beginning
of this whole high domicile,

meridians alive for all to feel.
Yes you, transparent crescent
of becoming, as the gateway
to the liminal horizon, as
messenger of the not yet born.

PRAYER

Please accept this prayer,
Allow the milk of it to take you
to the coming together of rivers,
to the place where you can bathe

at night in the shy faithfulness
of stars, to the meadow you
will traverse, safe, to discover
on the other edge the forgiveness

in the moist breath of a leaping stag,
the whole world held still alive
in his antlers. In that moment,
out of darknesses, may you follow

the scent of yellow, knowing
that it too will die. May you be
a person I love who still lives
in bare toes tasting grass arising.

Please, say this with me now.

TURQUOISE PRAYER OF SPRING

What if the turquoise prayer of Spring
was an almost hidden window,
opened only once a year,
inviting yellow peeper breezes
with their nostril dance of waftings
to free us from our ice cube selves?

I would look right through that window
to where the green becomes from,
and like a dried up glob of clay
I would swallow all that water-breath
and forget about the mailbox
as for once I understood what it means
to be dew.

I would look right through that window
to pinkish trees across the river,
to where frogs receive communion
and manure meets the moon,
and woodcocks know their purpose.

I would be ambushed by the budding
as I listened through the window,
and I would taste at last the sap
of how the music happens.

MY LIFE WITH LEWY

My Life with Lewy

by Alexander Dreier

IN THE SUMMER OF 2014, on an early morning walk near our cabin on an island off the coast of Maine, where I was enjoying a solitary retreat, I came upon a group of indigenous looking children dressed in clothes made of leaves. Ignoring my greeting, they followed me right into the house where their apparent ringleader, a three-foot tall man with dreadlocks, who appeared to have a hose coming out of his head, was engaging a group of adults in some kind of ritual. Fascinated as I was by their ceremonies, which also involved magical screens and spinning trees, I eventually called the local sheriff to have them removed from the property. It was by then after 10 PM. They had long overstayed their welcome and obstinately refused to respond to my most basic questions: "Who are you? Why are you here? What are you doing?" The next day my wife, Olivia, and my brother-in-law arrived and finally convinced me that my day-long interactions with this strange cast of characters had all been a very long "waking dream."

Hallucinations can, in fact, be a hallmark of Lewy body disease, the progressive neurological disorder I was diagnosed with in the fall of 2012. As described by my neurologist, small clusters of protein, called Lewy bodies, form in neurons in the brain and elsewhere in the body. They block the production of neurotransmitter substances and alter the functioning of the brain in a variety of ways, eventually leading to dementia and death. Fortunately for me, the course of my illness appears to be relatively gradual. The intensity and duration of the hallucinatory experience described above, and in much more detail in the poem entitled, "What Happened," was likely exacerbated by a temporary imbalance in the mix of medicines that I take on a daily basis. These medicines help me to make the best use of whatever neurotransmitter substances are available to my brain, supporting cognition and keeping me grounded, as much as possible, in consensual reality. More often, my hallucinatory experiences are fleeting in nature, more like momentary illusions. At the far edge of our field, winter branches may for an instant become Olivia's grandfather, looking distinguished in a three-piece tweed suit. In a gentle breeze, our willow tree might become a troop of dancers. A granite boulder on the coast of Maine may look just like a hippopotamus enjoying an afternoon nap, while a cloud takes on the exact physiognomy of Winston Churchill. And, for the last four years, mailboxes commonly appear as people of all shapes, sizes, and sorts.

A number of poems in this volume were written after my 2012 diagnosis; others were written over the previous decade. My neurologist suspects my condition was likely brewing ever since I lost my sense of smell at age forty, over twenty-five years ago. While I have always had a mind that revels in odd juxtapositions and irreverent humor, I strongly believe that Lewy body disease has enhanced my creativity, encouraging me to stretch beyond the boundaries of ordinary perception. Given that the symptoms have grown stronger in recent years, understanding my diagnosis and accepting that my brain is changing have been hugely important, keeping my feet on the ground, as I allow Lewy body to crack open new ways of seeing.

My first inkling that something was strangely amiss occurred a full year before my 2012 diagnosis. One evening as I was driving home, approaching a well-lit railway bridge underpass, I was stunned to see a large animal calmly lumber off the curb. As I slammed on my brakes, I distinctly saw an alligator directly ahead of me. In the several seconds that it took me to bring the car to a complete halt, I realized that oddly, I had not experienced any of the sudden jolt that usually accompanies a collision. As I looked around, I saw no animal of any kind and reminded myself that I was in downtown Amherst, Massachusetts, hardly the habitat of large reptiles. After a few more blinks, I assured myself that there was no alligator or anything resembling one, only a man in a car whose sense of reality had just received more of a jolt than the one he had expected from a collision under a railway bridge.

Perhaps I should have been a little less surprised by this event, given that Olivia and I had just returned from a vacation on the coast of Maine, during which the experience of more momentary illusions had begun, usually in the form of animated figures or features appearing on the surfaces of the natural world. For example, while paddling with Olivia in a canoe, I constantly directed her attention to curved lines or shapes in the granite outcroppings at the ocean's edge that seemed to me to be impossibly human-made. To my surprise, she did not see what I saw, such as a large, artistic rendering of Richard Nixon's distinctive face, jowls and all, nor did she appreciate the aesthetically stunning outline of a polar bear along a broad granite surface. Other animal-like shapes emerged from decaying trees, partially covered by moss or draped with lichen. To be sure, I had no doubt that what I saw were rocks, trees, and lichens. Well, I did have some doubt, and at the same time felt privy to a normally unseen aspect of the natural world. But the alligator crossing the road in Amherst—that was simply too much! And so before allowing myself to abandon the few cords of rationality that still tethered me to some sort of grounding, I resorted to one of my favorite sources of wisdom, known to most of the world as Google. Within two hours of scanning the web, I concluded that I likely had something called Lewy body disease. Visual illusions, hallucinations, problems with processing complex instructions, and numerous other symptoms all matched my own, and so I made an appointment to see a neurologist at a nearby teaching hospital. While I realized that Lewy body was a progressive neurological disorder that no rational person would wish upon themselves, the idea that I might soon have a real diagnosis was somewhat exciting, as my adult life had been full of seemingly mysterious symptoms that sapped my energy, but never gelled into a clear diagnosis, let alone an effective treatment.

My Journey to Diagnosis

At about age forty, while working on a psychiatric ward, I began noticing unpleasant odors, undetected by others. A few months later I lost my sense of smell altogether and then gradually developed debilitating fatigue, often accompanied by the sensation that I was coming down with the flu, though the flu never quite materialized. The catch-all diagnosis for such a cluster of symptoms at the time was Chronic fatigue syndrome, believed in by some medical practitioners and scorned by others.

As I continued in my training as a psychologist, I could not help wondering if my symptoms reflected some deep-seated neurosis. After all, I never did get the flu. Maybe I was just lazy or lacking in will forces, needed more vitamins or less carbohydrates, or could it be that I was out of touch with my life's true mission, one that would eventually engage and energize the whole of me, if only I knew what it was? However, neither intensive self-examination nor faddish health regimes made the symptoms go away. The fatigue persisted and persisted, accompanying—and often undermining—the various ventures I took on in life: caring for the livestock on our small family homestead; co-founding and working as a therapist in an alternative, community-based program for those in psychological distress; co-creating a comedy improv troupe (the Villa Jidiots) and a company (Net Mirth) that aimed to bring levity into organizational life; performing comedic monologues that used my life experiences and some of their absurdities as a platform for musings on life's mysteries; and writing poetry.

Being in the role of "patient" with an unknown diagnosis easily leads one to become the object of all sorts of theories, not to mention the nostrums offered by all manner of enthusiastic healers, ranging from wonderfully skilled conventional physicians to folk healers, faith healers, surveyors of magical devices, and shamanic channelers of spiritual energies, to name a few. Naturally curious and willing to try almost anything, I offered myself up to quite a range of practitioners. Some on the alternative side of the spectrum promised a panacea, a cure for all that ailed me. When none appeared, the failure was often blamed on me, the patient, with the suggestion that I was resisting, holding on to some deep-set pattern that I was unwilling to relinquish.

The idea of some that perhaps nothing at all was wrong with me, while provocative, also matched my own sense that whether my actual diagnosis was Chronic fatigue, Lyme disease, or gluten intolerance, my journey towards healing would require stretching into a deeper self-acceptance. I might also need to embrace the degree to which illness is often incomprehensible, despite our best efforts at a rock solid diagnosis, a "gnosis" that suggests a clear-cut treatment plan.

In truth, my journey to diagnosis for a long time consisted of the nothingness of empty speculative and ineffectual labels. Ironically, my first most "real" symptom was a non-existent alligator. It manifested as an obstacle in my path, but actually allowed me to take my first substantial step forward in a twenty-year process of trying to understand what was wrong with me. Before the non-existent alligator, I was like countless patients who are dismissed because of the vague, ephemeral nature of their illness, who are not "believed." Paradoxically, the hallucination of an alligator suggested something that should be detectable by any knowledgeable neurologist, and so I eagerly awaited my appointment at a nearby teaching hospital.

Unfortunately, what I thought was a very believable

hallucination was met with a fair degree of disbelief. The neurologist made it clear that he found me far too articulate, witty, and "normal" for anything to be pathologically wrong. The notion that I might have Lewy body disease was quickly dismissed. However, to appease what I think he saw as an overly worried baby boomer, the neurologist ordered some neuropsychological testing, an MRI, and a CAT scan, all of which took months to schedule. The neuro-psych tests consisted of quite entertaining word games and puzzles designed to detect hidden evidence of flaws in cognition or cerebral functioning. Some six months later, the neurologist called to say that something was indeed wrong with me. The tests showed that my verbal acuity was intact, but my visuospatial processing was amiss, and according to the scan, some parts of my brain might be atrophying. His conclusion was that I was in an early stage of Alzheimer's disease, for which (in his opinion) there was no treatment other than a few medicines of dubious efficacy for anyone other than the stockholders of pharmaceutical companies.

Needless to say, the diagnosis came as a shock, nor were Olivia and I convinced of its accuracy, having watched my mother go through Alzheimer's disease with a very different set of symptoms. I had no particular difficulty with memory, nor had I ever become disoriented or lost in familiar surroundings. Moreover, these curious hallucinations were continuing. I would frequently see a person over my left shoulder or a furry animal scurrying across the living room floor. I continued to raise the possibility of Lewy body disease with the neurologist, but he was more than dubious, and I suspected at this point that I had read more on the disease than he had.

I had also grown curious about the implications of a sleep disorder that I had developed several years earlier. It bears the acronym of RBD and the full name of Rapid eye movement sleep behavior disorder. In RBD, a mechanism in the brain stem fails to cause bodily paralysis during REM sleep (the dream state) with the result that the dreamer begins to physically act out his or her dream, often somewhat dangerously so, as my wife can attest. The dreams seem to emanate from the part of the brain concerned with fight / flight response and so frequently involve being attacked, and attacking back. RBD, I learned, is one of several parasomnias, a category of sleep disorders that feature getting stuck somewhere between sleep and wakefulness. I also discovered new research indicating that RBD is often a precursor of Lewy body disease. As far as I could tell, my constellation of symptoms pointed strongly towards Lewy body disease, not Alzheimer's. As I continued to review the literature, I kept encountering the name of Dr. Bradley Boeve, a leading researcher in Lewy body disease and a practicing neurologist at the Mayo Clinic in Rochester, Minnesota.

I contacted the clinic and, following their instructions, prepared an exhaustive review of all my symptoms, history, diagnoses—everything concerning my patienthood for the past twenty plus years. Given Dr. Boeve's international reputation, I worried whether my case would be of sufficient interest, and the process felt something like applying to a top college. Some six months later, and well over a year after the encounter with the alligator, I learned that I had been accepted, and Dr. Boeve had an opening to see me. As soon as I entered the gracious atrium of the Mayo Clinic, where live classical music welcomes and midwestern warmth abounds, I felt received. In fact, I burst into tears, as I also suffer from yet another odd neurological symptom known as Pseudobulbar affect, which manifests as a tendency to cry or laugh at unexpected moments and is often secondary to brain injury, dementia, or other neurological conditions. I apparently share this one with conservative Congressman, John Boehner, but I trust the comparison ends there.

The Mayo Clinic is renowned for its holistic approach to medicine. There is no jumping to quick conclusions. Specialists work as a collaborative team to uncover the root causes of whatever symptoms are presented. As I met with Dr. Boeve and his colleagues, I was struck by their genuine interest in all I could share, including the occasional sound of coins jingling in my head, which is apparently known as "Exploding head syndrome" (I am not making this up). I felt that I was in the hands of highly skilled medical virtuosos, committed to the highest standards of diagnosis and healing. After a series of tests and scans, Dr. Boeve confirmed what "Dr. Google" and I had concluded some fourteen months earlier: I do have Lewy body disease! It is a progressive neurological disorder related to Parkinson's disease, in which small balls of protein called, "Lewy bodies," form in the brain's neurons, blocking the production of the neurotransmitter substances that allow nerve impulses to cross from one end of a synapse to another. As a result, the disease affects the entire neurochemistry of the brain. The cause is unknown. Frequently, its symptoms have led to an assumption of Alzheimer's disease, but its etiology is totally distinct, and it is now recognized as the second leading cause of dementia. Unlike in Alzheimer's disease, the neurons themselves are not dying, and so medicines that keep the neurotransmitter substances in the synapses as long as possible can have a dramatic effect on symptoms, even if they do not halt progression of the underlying pathology. In Parkinson's disease, these little balls of protein first affect the motor neurons. In Lewy body disease they first enter the inmost layers of the brain, especially affecting those parts of the brain concerned with visuospatial processing and so-called executive functioning, hence the visual illusions and hallucinations as well as the fact that I no longer seem to have the smarts to tell my smart phone what to do. Usually the disease comes on suddenly in the patient's sixties, but Dr. Boeve believes that there is another form that develops early and progresses slowly. In my case, the loss of smell at age forty was most likely the first sign, and the fatigue I have experienced for a large part of my adult life, a primary symptom.

My Life with Lewy

What is it like to live with Lewy on a daily basis? In my experience things that are ordinary often become extraordinary. This then presents me with an invitation to encounter that extraordinariness in whatever ways I am able or willing. Sometimes I am startled, even scared, by highly unusual sights that I cannot immediately identify. At other moments, especially when I am a passenger in a car, I can be heard to exclaim one of my most used phrases, "What is that?" My visual illusions vary according to the quantity of ambient light, the weather, sounds, whom I am with, etc. When they solidify into images, they can become prompts for poetry.

The medicines I now take keep this often surprising imagery at a level where it mostly does not alarm me but rather, in all kinds of interesting ways, leads me to question what I am seeing. I do have difficulty working with the normal dimensions of time as they are presented in calendars, and just how to operate my laptop is becoming increasingly veiled in mystery. This cluster of challenges carries the medical label of "mild cognitive impairment." My neural pathways are gradually functioning with less linearity than is considered normal. From a medical perspective, the visual illusions are a form of apophenia, the seeing of patterns that make sense out of meaningless data, meaningless because of some malfunctioning in the visuospatial part of my brain. Similarly, the tendency to see faces or images in everyday objects carries the medical term, "pareidolia," and is often used to explain the visions claimed by religious seekers. No doubt the train of my thinking, or the ways in which I link percept with concept, is no longer restricted to very prescribed tracks, though in my case, I am not sure it ever was. While at times this can result in some confusion, I believe it has also cracked open my capacity to see with more creativity and perhaps with more depth.

When Lewy body arrived in my body, it seemed that it came to stay. Who is this unexpected guest and how many of its microscopic little balls have accompanied him? My immediate response was to try to send him away, back to where he came from, but as I have worked on acceptance and observed the accompanying silver lining of creativity, the imagery has responded in kind. There was a time two years ago when visions of reptiles became more prevalent, and I sometimes awoke at night to discover the room full of spiders and snakes. Then one day, I noticed a girl standing at the edge of the woods holding the hand of a much younger child. The girl wore a shabby tunic of rough cloth and had one arm raised. What caught my attention was the feeling of welcome or even hospitality that seemed to emanate from the child, as if she was delivering a message that there was nothing to fear. The figure remained for months, and I never approached it, preferring to allow for some kind of unspoken conversation, avoiding my frequent impulse to pull out my binoculars in order to answer my usual question of "what the heck is that?"

As a person fascinated by words, their meanings, and the expansion of their meanings, I consider myself (at least in my best moments) to be somewhat blessed to have a long term relationship with a "condition" such as Lewy body disease that constitutes a limitless font of fresh ways to experience alternative presentations of the world. Every day I encounter another possibility of seeing, hearing, or simply observing some object that presents itself in a cloak of newness that radiates previously unknown features or knowings. Where yesterday there was a stout old apple tree in the orchard, today I notice a large-bottomed middle-aged dancer of indeterminate gender, seemingly engaged in a rhythmic, gestural symphony with unseen companions.

Is this illness? Am I projecting a different world into yours? Is my seeing any more or less real than the world of a child catching a frog in a cloud view? It is not necessarily easy to shift between these worlds or live with these questions. My experience suggests that balance comes not only with accepting what flows through the neuronal streams of Lewy, but also with the right medicine appearing in the right moment through the creativity of right diagnosis. Illness, it seems, is best addressed by working *with* it, not against it, through a collaborative relationship between physician and patient. What lies at the heart of my illness remains a mystery both to me and to medical science, and yet my daily life is richly full of synaptic surprises.

My son, Lucas, has been living and working with a remarkable indigenous group called the Kogi who live in northern Colombia on the highest coastal mountain in the world. Numbering between 15,000 and 20,000, they are widely considered the most intact pre-Colombian civilization extant. Their society is led by priests, known as "Mamas" who manage all aspects of Kogi life, including their deeply ecological approach to agriculture and efforts to live in harmony with both the natural world and what they experience as the world of spirit. The Mamas undergo rigorous training in contemplative practices, some spending extensive periods of time in the dark, to enhance their faculties of inner seeing. The Kogi are quite reclusive, and in their daily life, boundaries with other worlds appear thin, not so different from my experience with life with Lewy.

It was dusk as we sat with the Mama of the village where Lucas lives. A small fire burned, throwing all manner of shadows on the walls of the surrounding huts, which displayed the animated shapes I have grown accustomed to. Before concluding our evening's exchange, I could not resist briefly describing my experiences with Lewy in order to ask the Mama if he could shed light on them. His response was immediate, "Do not be afraid, this is Aluna (loosely translated as "the spiritual dimensions") allowing you to see her aliveness."

Afterword

by Bradley F. Boeve, MD

I AM HONORED to write an afterword for this remarkable book of poems authored by such a remarkable man.

I am hoping that, by describing here a "big picture" view of the brain, and then narrowing this picture to a particular disease with obscure boundaries, detailing the brain's innate ability to resist/adapt to disease, and then applying these concepts to Alexander Dreier's creativity over many years as revealed in his poetry, I will be able to underscore the uniqueness of this publication and its meanings.

As trite as this may sound, the brain is truly an amazing organ, with 100 billion cells (known as neurons) which must work in concert for humans to function independently and thrive. We take it for granted when the ensemble of neurons, which neurologists refer to as neuronal networks, function in sync such that cognition, behavior, motor functioning, sleep, etc., are all normal. There are several issues and questions relating to brain functioning. To specify only a few: What constitutes normal versus abnormal? or sanity versus psychosis? What neuronal networks are involved in the most basic of animal behaviors such as wakefulness and sleep? What networks are involved in appreciating or expressing the more complex aspects of human functioning relating to creativity/art, empathy/sympathy, humor, sarcasm, disgust, and the like? And when brain functioning becomes abnormal due to disease, are most neuronal networks affected? Does brain disease imply that only negative consequences can result? Stated in different terms, are most aspects of brain functioning this or that, or black or white, or positive or negative? If so, this implies that there are sharp distinctions or boundaries between these dichotomies. Or are there indistinct boundaries (i.e., shades of gray) for many aspects of brain functioning?

What happens in the brain during one of the more common diseases of later life—Lewy body disease (LBD)? While the precise pathophysiologic processes involved in LBD are not clear, this disorder is associated with the accumulation of clumps of alpha-synuclein protein in neurons, and degrees of dysfunction of many neurotransmitter systems and key groups of neurons explain many of the cardinal features. When the networks in the deeper structures of the brain known as the basal ganglia (where the neurotransmitter known as dopamine is active) are primarily affected, the symptoms are usually those of Parkinson's disease. Mild cognitive impairment (MCI) or dementia (often termed dementia with Lewy bodies or DLB) as well as visual hallucinations, illusions, etc., is manifested when the groups of neurons in the limbic system and neocortex are primarily affected. Memory and insight are largely preserved in LBD. Many individuals with LBD develop changes in smell and sleep years or even decades prior to the onset of cognitive, behavioral, or motor symptoms.

Let's explore the sleep-related aspects of LBD and other neurologic disorders further. There are networks in the brain which control the three "states of being" among many animal beings—wakefulness, rapid eye movement (REM) sleep, and non-REM sleep. These networks are tightly controlled so that in the normal adult, an individual is in one and only one of these states—usually for hours at a time. During wakefulness, a person is obviously awake and has normal muscle tone so that arm and leg movements are possible. During REM sleep, there is active suppression of muscle tone such that a person is largely paralyzed, and this is the stage of sleep when dreaming typically occurs. In the neurologic disorder known as narcolepsy, there is disruption in the tight control of the sleep states such that boundaries are less defined, resulting in unpleasant intrusions of REM sleep phenomena into wakefulness which is manifested as sleep attacks, visual hallucinations, and suppression of muscle tone known as sleep paralysis and cataplexy. Aspects of wakefulness can also invade into REM sleep, resulting in normal muscle tone while dreaming such that individuals can appear to be "acting out one's dreams" (this is called "REM sleep behavior disorder"). Narcolepsy (also called "status dissociatus") is therefore a striking example of a dissociation of the states of being. There is growing evidence that some of these same networks may be dysfunctional in LBD, which could explain the fatigue/daytime sleepiness, visual hallucinations, and REM sleep behavior disorder so common in this disease. LBD and narcolepsy therefore represent fascinating (but debilitating) brain disorders where sleep-wake state boundaries are blurred. Furthermore, visual hallucinations and delusions are often thought to represent features of "psychosis"—being out of touch with reality—and the term "insanity" is sometimes applied. In those with LBD, the delusions often sound like reasonable interpretations of the visual perceptions (e.g., believing that little people in the home have malicious intent). But if some visual hallucinations reflect intrusions of dream imagery (i.e., the percept), and the delusions represent the psyche's attempts to make sense of the visual perceptions (i.e., the concept), then how does one differentiate features of status dissociatus from psychosis? This is another example of the blurring of brain/mind boundaries.

Let's also ponder some of the most highly complex aspects of human cognition and behavior. Appreciating and expressing creativity through writing, painting, sculpting, acting, music, etc., requires some basic skills and emotional investment. Some individuals appear gifted from a young age, and many hone their skills over time through practice, seeking more exposure to audible or visual stimuli, introspection, and conversation, among other activities. Empathy and sympathy are instinctual in some ways, and these seem to be well-developed at an early age and are difficult to modify with age. Humor/wit/sarcasm are also complex features, with many individuals seemingly blessed with these abilities when young. Exhibiting comedic expression often takes the form of telling jokes or responding comedically in the to and fro of oral communication. Oral cadence and inflections of words, along with facial expressions and other forms of body language, combine to make others laugh. The neural substrates for these complex brain abilities are diffuse, but most behaviors involve networks in the frontal and temporal lobes.

There is a pervasive perception that degenerative brain diseases such as LBD, Alzheimer's disease, and frontotemporal dementia results in progressive degeneration of most or all neuronal networks. Some of the networks in the frontal regions, and particularly the parietal and occipital neuronal networks, are affected in LBD. The images of relatives, friends, and celebrities who have endured these disorders seemingly emphasize a universally negative view, thereby contributing to the dread of those who are older but do not have any cognitive/behavioral/motor/sleep symptoms. Yet there are many examples of individuals who have found enhanced abilities and other positive aspects despite a degenerative brain disorder. In fact, there are many documented individuals with no apparent gifts or interests in the creative arts during decades of living "normally," who then begin experiencing a decline in memory, language, complex visual processing, or motor functioning as part of the degenerative brain disease, and their creative expression blossoms. Some have created remarkable stories, poems, paintings, sculptures—thereby shattering the notion that all is negative in progressive brain diseases. These spontaneous expressions of creative blossoming *despite* the presence of a brain disease reflect the brain's innate ability to mold and seemingly resist (or at least adapt to) degeneration.

I had the great pleasure of meeting Alexander Dreier and his lovely wife Olivia several years ago. Like many resourceful individuals with troubling symptoms and diagnoses from clinicians that did not jive, he sought guidance from "Dr. Google" and made an accurate self-diagnosis. Further clinical assessment and diagnostic studies supported the diagnosis of LBD. Many of his clinical features, astutely and humorously described in some of his poems and in his essay "My Life with Lewy," are typical of this disorder. Some of his symptoms are as representative of the blurring of brain and mind boundaries as anyone has experienced, yet his uncanny insightfulness and wit add to the imagery and thoughtfulness of his writings. His enduring approach to life is an inspiration.

I do not mean to minimize the challenges that LBD poses to individuals and their families. Yet adapting to these challenges, and maintaining meaning in life, can be done with courage, humor, optimism, and creativity as reflected by Mr. Dreier's approach and writings. We are fortunate to be able to enjoy his poetry. I am fortunate to have grown to know him.

BRADLEY F. BOEVE, MD is a Board-certified physician specializing in Neurology, Behavioral Neurology and Neuropsychiatry, and Sleep Medicine.